How to Start A Successful

CLEANING

BUSINESS

The Essential Guide To Starting A Cleaning Business

Kim Robertson

2nd Edition

Table of Contents

Chapter 1 First Things First

"Taking Care of Business before Getting into Business"

Before you get started, obtain a notebook dedicated to your new business. Your notebook will become your best friend when it comes to keeping track of information, pricing, thoughts, and for general note taking. Keep your new pal handy.

If you choose to incorporate, you can do it yourself online for between two and three hundred dollars.

If you choose to do it yourself "DIY," visit a CPA (certified public accountant) and get their advice or help with the process. Google search for accountants in your neighborhood and make sure you are talking to a qualified CPA— not just a bookkeeper. Bookkeepers keep books, but they may not be required to follow the same legal standards as CPAs.

You will also need a federal ID number, which can be handled at the same time as the incorporating process online. There is a small fee for this service. Until you get a federal ID number, you will have to use your social security number in this dealing. I chose a Subchapter S corporation, and for me, this was an excellent choice, but you may decide to go with an LLC. Subchapter S-tax status and LLC corporations are in my opinion a much better way for you to begin your new business. There are tax benefits and legal protections that you will receive by choosing either one of these. One of the most undeniable gains is that you will not pay self- employment tax on your gross revenues which is at present $13.30 per hundred dollars of your business bank deposits. Speaking to a certified public accountant will give you a solid understanding of the benefits and protections that either the S-corp or the LLC provide. Since I am not a CPA or an attorney I cannot advise you, and it is more complex than I have described here – yet an- other reason that you need help in making an informed, educated decision.

A DBA is an individual 'doing business as.' For example, let's say your name is Mary Jones and you decide to go into business by purchasing a business license LLC. The DBA, in my opinion, is something to be avoided.

Make the decision and establish your legal name, then proceed to the occupational license and the insurance. If you are trying to create a startup budget ahead of time, talk to your new CPA and ask for the license and insurance information from both the insurance company and the payroll service first to determine your costs. I am assuming that if you bought this report, you have decided to forge ahead, want to do everything correctly, and are ready to go.

Another thing to talk to your accountant or CPA about is tangible and nontangible taxes. Some areas have taxes for the equipment that you own, your desk and vacuum cleaners for example. It is usually inexpensive, but you need to get the facts.

Chapter 2: License(s)

Like it or not, if you want to be a legal cleaning service, you will most likely need an occupational license. Different towns, cities, and municipalities call the license by various names. My area calls the license a 'business tax receipt.'

Licensing is another thing I would discuss with a local CPA or small business advisor. You may need a separate license for both the city and the county that you plan to conduct business in. If you are going to do business in any neighboring towns, a permit will be required for each city where you intend to conduct business.

A janitorial license is required for cleaning homes and offices. When talking to your advisor, please be specific about what type of cleaning you intend to do to make sure you have issued the appropriate type of license. For example, if you intend to add pressure cleaning to your offered services, you may need a special contractor's license.

Keep in mind some licenses are obtained through your state, not just your county or city. Your county will keep this part of your license in their files. Without this documentation, you will not be able to retrieve, maintain, or manage any license for that particular type of cleaning. This is why you must be very specific about your intentions with your CPA, your license department, and your insurance company.

So gather all of your information, make a final decision about the types of cleaning you intend to offer, and get licensed.

Chapter 3: Banking

Without any delay, you need to visit a few banks and establish a new business checking account. Remember I said "visit." In other words, shop around for the bank that suits your purpose. Arm yourself with the paperwork and all information required, but make your decision using a simple two-step process: Compare the pros and cons of each bank's offer as well as each account offer.

This is no time to play favorites as banking fees can add up quickly. Not only that, but depending on what each bank offers for each account, you can also save time each month and at years end with your bookkeeping. In the beginning, you may have a monthly fee if starting off with a low monthly balance as is common with new businesses. However, if you've done your homework, you may find a new bank opening up in your neighborhood that has little to no fee despite the low balance.

You may also discover that if you have more than one account at a bank, one of the accounts could be complimentary. Things like monthly fees, overdraft fees, ATM cards, and a company credit card can make the whole experience easier. It's not a bad idea to have all of your payments, charges, debits, and checks printed out each month on one statement. This can be a considerable saving at years end when providing paperwork to your CPA.

So shop around and share the information gathering process with your new accountant. Their input will help you understand what they will need from you at years end. This information can help you make an informed decision about the bank and the services that best suits your business.

Chapter 4: Insurance

Next, I will discuss the differences between using an insurance company and going through a payroll service. This is rather involved so reread it as many times as you require. I also use strong verbiage about what you should and should not do for a reason. I am assuming you are trying to operate a legitimate company and you are not trying to skirt the rules or cheat the system. When you manage your business the right way, you will never have to worry about "what could happen if..."

The choice remains yours solely.

You should make some calls to a few different insurance companies. If you have friends that own small businesses, ask them who their insurance is with. You will discover that many small businesses have their insurance at one of just a few companies available in your area.

Some insurance companies have payment plans while others do not. I believe those that offer payment plans will always be the most popular, but as long as the insurance carrier is A-rated (which means they are likely to pay a claim should you have one), the choice as to who you purchase your coverage from is up to you.

The prices may or may not vary, but you will learn some important things along the way. For instance, there can easily be a two or three hundred dollar difference in price because your insurance underwriter charges a fee to write up your policy. Yes, the paperwork process is how they make some of their money — they get paid just to sign you up.

When you place your first call, tell them in detail what kind of services you will offer your clients. You may have decided back during the licensing process to change some of your offerings. If not, then this is another place where you may want to delete those extra services. Not offering certain services now does not mean you never will; just get started, and focus on your greatest strengths and skills. Start making some money and then add in those services later. By the time you are ready, you will have a solid customer base to work with.

Insurance companies will ask for your projected payroll to help determine how much the insurance will cost. If you are just starting out and you have only a few clients lined up (or zero as of this reading), ask the insurance agent what the minimum payroll amount is for which they will write the policy.

The minimum is around thirty or thirty-five thousand dollars. This means that your payroll can be somewhere between thirty and thirty-five thousand dollars for the year. For example, if you pay yourself thirty thousand dollars in salary for a thirty-five thousand dollar plan, you will not owe an additional premium at the end of the policy period.

However, if you pay yourself thirty-six thousand dollars, you will owe an additional premium on whatever portion of the payroll goes over the covered amount — in this case, you are over by one thousand dollars, and will pay accordingly. If you pay yourself less then you will not get a refund, since there was a minimum payroll amount. This is something that you want to keep in mind as your business grows.

If you begin with only yourself as an employee, and later find the need to hire someone, it would be better to pick up the phone and tell your insurance agent right away than to receive a large bill after the audit. What is an audit? An audit is simply this — if your insurance policy starts on February 14th and ends the following

February 14th, you will either receive a phone call, a letter, or both as the insurance company wants to evaluate your payroll. They are looking into your records or books for what you paid yourself and your employees. Based on these numbers, you will either owe additional premium or not.

Now for the general liability coverage you need. Even if you are a small company, I would suggest asking for at least five hundred thousand dollars of coverage. However, keep in mind that offices and larger jobs will probably want to see at least a million dollars of general liability coverage. Consider obtaining increased coverage as you grow, as this will protect you and your client. Furthermore, increased coverage will get you considered for positions that may turn you down with a smaller policy. A typical janitorial service usually carries a minimum of two million dollars in general liability coverage, two million in business auto coverage plus worker's comp (compensation) coverage. Larger companies tend to carry ten to fifteen million dollars in coverage.

As stated above, the auditor will visit you and ask to see all of your payroll figures. These figures will tell them how much you paid both yourself and others, and they can then determine whether you owe additional money.

Make sure to ask each insurance company that you visit if they write worker's comp insurance since not all companies do.

Different states are very different about worker's comp requirements, and some require comp if you have just one employee, so you must ask both your insurance agent and the place where you obtained your license for worker's comp requirements.

The Chamber of Commerce or SBA in your area may also be of help in determining needs. Violation of the worker's comp requirement could land you in somber legal trouble.

CAUTION: NEVER USE SUBCONTRACTORS THAT DO NOT HAVE INSURANCE OF THEIR OWN, BECAUSE YOUR INSURANCE COMPANY WILL EITHER CANCEL YOUR POLICY, OR

YOUR BILL WILL BE A BIG SURPRISE —
ONE THAT YOU WILL NOT ENJOY.

If you have a million dollars' worth of
general liability, then each subcontractor
must have at least the same amount, or you
will end up paying the difference. Always,
and I always stress, make subcontractors
provide proof of their insurance (IN
WRITING!), and never, ever (and I mean
NEVER, EVER) take their word for it.

Get a copy of their license and a copy of their
insurance papers and hold onto them, as you
will need to prove that they had insurance
on the dates that they were on jobs for you
that you paid them for. If you hired them for
work on January 12th, and their insurance
policy start date is January 13th, then guess

who pays in case of an incident? Keep their paperwork close as audits come after your policy period. You may potentially need to save their license and insurance paperwork for at least thirteen months.

Make each subcontractor obtain an insurance certificate with you as the certificate holder. To make sure that the insurance certificate is not bogus have the insurance certificate emailed, mailed, or faxed to you from their insurance company. Do not accept a copy that they have brought to you. It is very easy for someone to create a bogus certificate. Also, and this is the most important part — your company needs to be listed as additional insured on the subcontractor's insurance certificate. If you get lazy about this fine print, you will pay, and you can only look in the mirror for whom to blame. It could also provoke you to lose your insurance and find yourself in the middle of a lawsuit. This is serious business — do not ignore this warning. Remember that you are responsible for your subcontractor's actions as well as your own. Any problem or lawsuit will come back to you for bad work they do or damage they cause.

Chapter 5: Payroll Service

Along with insurance companies, payroll services can fulfill many of your business needs. There are a plethora of payroll services available to you, and a quick Google search is good enough to get you started. As the name implies, payroll services handle your payroll, the reports that the government requires, and the stuff that keeps you on the more comfortable side of jail bars.

Most, if not all, payroll services can sell you general liability insurance, worker's comp, and business auto insurance. They will produce your W-2 forms at the end of the tax year for each of your employees and yourself, plus — and this is so helpful — those insurance audits can be handled with a simple phone call. Additionally, they take care of all of the crazy record keeping of employee salaries.

The way the payroll process works is that you start by tracking your employee's hours, and call or email the payroll service either weekly or biweekly. Your payroll service will then process the paychecks for you. They calculate and collect all the taxes, collect their fee, take care of insurance and mail or direct deposit the checks. Each quarter (four times per year) they also provide to the government all the tax reporting requirements, and taxes collected for the state and federal government, and again at the end of the year — and all you did was make a few phone calls to report your payroll totals. For you, this means no messy tax paperwork, no massive government paperwork, and streamlined record keeping.

The other beauty of the payroll service is that the insurance is pay-as-you-go instead of the immediate out of pocket expense accrued through regular insurance companies. The payroll service will add up the wages, taxes, general liability insurance, worker's comp, and their fees. You then have one debit from your account. Again, they will either mail the checks to you or do direct deposit for each employee, and each employee can choose what they prefer. More pluses of the payroll service are that they will provide employment applications, minimum wage charts, and worker's compensation injury reporting charts that are required by the government.

You may be considering saving money so that you will do the payroll yourself. To put things in perspective, my last payroll company only charged me forty-two dollars to process my payroll. That made a total of eighty-four dollars per month for what would have been multiple hours of work and a major hassle to take care of. The main reason I started using a payroll service is that ONE TIME I failed to mail an end of the year report to the government for my total payroll for the year. Prior to this, I had emailed four quarterly reports, paid all the tax, (and in fact, overpaid), but I forgot the end of the year report that had the totals for all four quarters. I mailed it in late, and the government gave me a fourteen hundred dollar penalty. I did not owe them a penny of tax, and I had emailed all four quarterly reports, but I failed to mail in the report that had all four reports combined for the year — because I simply missed it under a stack of papers. In sum, consider getting a payroll service and make sure they are reputable since their failure can come back to you. Ask around and check with the Better Business Bureau for ratings and recommendations.

So the options would be for you to handle all the insurance, tax responsibilities, reporting, check writing, and audits yourself or get a payroll service.

Chapter 6: Company Technology

It is better to have a designated company phone and fax line, but in today's technological world you also need internet access and an email address for your business. To keep things on the cheap side, use your current cell phone and answer it as if you are the secretary. Use your company name each and every time you answer your phone unless it is your mom.

Get an email address that complements your business name; xylocleans@gmail.com for example. Spend some time and get a catchy email address. Use the email as your faxing service. I had only one vendor that still used a fax — everyone else scanned and emailed. You may even fancy seeing into your web domain name and custom email address as your business grows.

Chapter 7: Printed Goodies

Once you have decided your company name and obtained your license, order some business cards. You need business cards with your name, phone number, email address and a few lines about the services you offer. Always place 'licensed and insured' on your cards, so that customers know you are serious about your work.

An inexpensive but great place to get cards made is online by a company called Vistaprint (vistaprint.com). Vistaprint has good prices, and they save your information for additional orders. Double and triple check your phone number, fax number, email address and the like and get those cards ordered. They offer many great products to meet your business needs. For example, they also have reasonably priced magnetic signs for your vehicle. The fancy stationary can wait for more profitable times, as well as the self-stick envelopes (I have no investment or connection to Vistaprint).

You also need a quote form, yes even for a residential cleaning job for the nice neighbor lady. You want to keep everybody playing nice, so write down your quote and give the customer a copy and keep a copy for yourself. I use a simple form sold by NEBS (nebs.com). The form Number that I found most useful was 6579, and it can be ordered with all of your company information printed on it. It includes a variety of great categories for general cleaning and there is space for notes. The form also comes in three parts, so you can give one to the customer, one to the employee doing the work, and keep one in your files.

Chapter 8: Advertising Ideas

Residential vs. Commercial

Have you given any thought to how you are going to get customers? Do you have an advertising budget to spend? I am going to assume your advertising budget is zero and that is fine. I was in business nearly thirty-six years made an amazing income and used word of mouth and shoe leather to grow my success.

Are you the type who is not shy and will approach anyone? I, of course, am not referring to people, who give you the creeps, but it is a real plus if you shed the shyness best you can. Start looking your best every time you leave the house — people form impressions long before you say hello. Tell everyone that comes within shouting distance about yourself and your company.

More importantly, show interest in others, and join some free groups — the knitting club, the fishing group — in short, network and do it fast. Take note of how many business cards you have in your pocket each day, because if you leave the house with twelve and come home with twelve, well what do you want me to say? Set your quota and pass those pretty cards out.

I will tell you that for me, the best dollars were made doing commercial cleaning, but residential cleaning does have its good points. If you want to make decent money —

somewhere between eight hundred and a thousand dollars per week — and want to have some real control over your clients and schedule, then go residential and light janitorial cleaning. On the other hand, if you want to have employees and operate your business in a few counties, then go commercial. I was commercial, and I operated my business in two counties. I would take an odd job out of town if the pay were right if I could handle it, and it was especially quiet in my normal area of operation.

A local newspaper ad may be a popular way to attract clients, but word of mouth is unbeatable. A happy customer will tell their friends and family and can vouch for the quality of your service. However, if you are going to advertise in the newspaper, Sunday papers have the largest readership. There is also the weekly paper with local coupons for you to target. Women tend to save both of these papers for the coupons, and most of your clients in residential service will be women.

You will have to put yourself out there to meet people, or it will take a long time to get anything worthwhile going. So start talking and passing out cards at the coffee shop, the grocery store, and the hair salon. Ask if you can place cards in businesses of the areas you are looking to target. Go back regularly to see if the cards need to be refilled.

If you do not yet know what to charge, you will have to do some research in your area.

Every town is different. While you are researching price, find out if the competition supplies their cleaning chemicals (more about supplying later). You will be able to earn a few bucks more if you supply and it is usually worth it.

Even in the cheapest areas, cleaners are getting fifteen to twenty dollars per hour. Anything less than that and you will be working some long hours to make a decent wage. In addition to the time spent cleaning, you also have to figure in the cost of gas, car insurance, and auto maintenance. If you are in a more depressed area, try offering a flat rate. Instead of twenty dollars per hour for a two-hour job, try quoting a forty-five dollar flat rate. If they like the idea of you bringing your supplies, quote it at fifty dollars. There will be some trial and error involved here, so negotiate as needed.

Another thing to watch out for is to not easily give in to the faces and smirks about your prices being too high — customers can be very cunning to get their way. If you are a fast, hard worker, you should be paid more than the types who shuffle around just to kill time and charge by the hour. If you are still having a tough time receiving the pricing you want and need, you can take a few of the cheaper jobs, BUT ONLY AS FILL IN.

As soon as possible get a better-paying client to replace the cheap client. Give them notice and do not look back. Your time is valuable and never forget that. That's right, you heard me, cut them loose and do not look back.

However, always remain professional and courteous when making the break.

Chapter 9: Meeting New Customers

When you visit a potential customer for the first time, you will want to find out what they are looking for and how often they will need your services. They will almost always say they are looking for weekly or biweekly service and they will want to know what that will cost. Now is the time to explain what you do as a 'general.' clean and ask if they have any additional special requests.

In a later chapter, I will provide you with a general scope of cleaning work, so you have something to go on. Some clients only want you to concentrate your efforts in some regions of the house such as their main bath, bedroom, and kitchen. Often they will delete second and third bedrooms and baths as the kids have moved away or are off to college. This is nothing to fret over, but note everything on your quote form, as you do not want to price out one thing and end up cleaning extra space. Selective amnesia runs rampant in cleaning customers.

Also, note that the first cleaning you perform will be more costly than the repeat cleans! Why? Because the house has probably not been cleaned in some time despite what the owner says to the contrary. So let us say the owner wants bi-weekly services and you are quoting the biweekly at seventy-five dollars per clean. The first clean could very well be one hundred to one hundred twenty-five dollars, and more if they want windows and appliances. Do that paperwork or get stung!

There are also those homeowners that say they want repeat services, but only want you to clean once — at the less expensive repeat service price. You will find out who is serious and who is not when you whip out your quote forms, and you give them a higher price for the first clean. If they do turn you down, you are probably better off anyway.

Another good practice is to adopt a minimum from the very start. Here is why: "Mrs. Nice Neighbor" wants to pay a low price, so she cons you into killing yourself cleaning her entire house for thirty-five dollars. As stated above, she says she wants regular repeat service, but only wants one cheap clean.

Good for her, lousy for you. First off, her house needs close to three hours of work, and second, you have to drive from her home to somewhere else before you are back on the clock and earning money. If you do decide to take her job, only do a reasonable amount of work for the thirty-five dollars. If she deems you are going to repeat this every week, she will use you until you drop.

You do not need customers like her, or they should be very short term. Break it off quick, or better yet, never take people like this for clients. They are abusive and downright cheap. So adopt a minimum such as setting a two-hour minimum for say forty-five dollars.

In our area, we can charge thirty to thirty-five dollars per hour. Do not forget your research as it is critical to your pricing structure.

Being cheaper just means you work just as hard for less money. Be smart. Aim to be the best and charge a competitive price — they will want you because of your excellent work. Remember, you are building a list of top quality clients and weeding out the undesirables takes some doing.

Chapter 10: Sticky Situations

Never clean refrigerators, ovens, or windows as part of your general cleaning package. Have the client schedule these ahead of your normal cleaning. For example, Ms. Smith's regular cleaning day is Mondays at 11:00 am. She wants the house done, but she has company coming, and the refrigerator is a mess. No problem. If you show up and she announces that she wants this done today "while you are here" that is your cue. Take control of the conversation right now.

Be very polite and say, "No trouble at all, I have a twenty dollar charge for cleaning refrigerators." It might even behoove you to have a quick peek inside the refrigerator before delivering your quote. If the fridge is a horror, change the fee to match! Sometimes, however, you simply do not have time to clean her home and add on the refrigerator because you have to get across town to your next client.

This type of situation is where things get touchy. Try to schedule the refrigerator for when you come again. If you do not, you could end up working double time to get the house done and the refrigerator cleaned for the same money. Many unsuspecting cleaners fall into this trap. The goal here is to get paid twenty to twenty-five dollars for a half-hour of your time instead of your normal rate, as this is a special money-making extra. Either way, I would say I have an extra charge for refrigerators, ovens, and windows, and if she does not want to pay it you, do not get cheated out of your service fee or end up cleaning her fridge for free.

Ovens are more like thirty-five to forty dollars depending on the condition. These can take as long as the rest of the house cleaning together, so price accordingly. If the oven is a disaster, charge according to how long you think it will take. Window cleaning has to be scheduled separately, as this is a much more time consuming task. Another option is to telephone the client that is scheduled after her and see if you could come a little later. You make extra money, and the clients are all kept happy.

Never let a client get you to throw in things like refrigerators and ovens. One of the perks of owning your own business is that you can charge more for the extras. Do not get duped. This is all part of the tasty cherry on top that you are working for. Another sneaky trick by clients is that they hire you to clean their house every week or every two weeks, but then when you are scheduled to go tomorrow, the homeowner calls to cancel and tells you to just come on your next scheduled date. Fine, but not so fast. When you show up on the next scheduled date, charge the client more than her normal fee. After all, it has now been double the length of time between regular cleanings, and the price you quoted was for the former scenario, not the current one. The work is heavier, and it will take longer.

The equation is easy: more work, more money. Do not let a client abuse you or it will not stop.

A client that is always canceling at the last minute costs you time and money. It is tough to fill a vacancy with little to no notice. Clients that do this repeatedly need to be replaced. Always be polite, and a replacement for their time-slot, and move on. This is your business, your livelihood, and you are building something here.

Undependable clients are as bad as undependable employees. These "Cancelling Carols" cost you money, keep your business from growing, and have an immediate impact on your take home pay. Get rid of them.

Chapter 11: Recap

Your clients chose you, and to be successful, and you must also choose them. Finding the right client is at least as important as advertising your business. You are looking to weed out the cheap, undependable, and difficult clients. Your productive working hours are limited, and to make your time count and to retain the value of your time you must choose the best customers.

Summary:

• See a CPA or visit your local SBA and decide how your business will be set up (DBA, Subchapter S corp, or LLC). Get your federal identification number at the same time.

- Ask questions about intangible taxes as well as if sales taxes are to be charged for your work.

Different areas differ in this regard.

- Obtain your business license for your county, city or both.

- Open a business checking account.

- Make those calls to an insurance company for the general liability insurance, the worker's compensation, and the business auto policy.

- Make calls to a few payroll companies and record all the facts about costs regarding the insurances, their fees for payroll processing, and all the services that they have to offer you.

- Make a decision about your phone.

- Set up an email address to compliment your new business name.

- Put a rush on those business cards. Triple check the information on your card before you approve it for mass printing since reprints take time.

- Don't forget to order a quote form. This is especially important.

- Hit the ground running even before your cards arrive. Tell everyone about your new business and its name.

• Follow up with as many of these people as possible when your cards arrive to get them on your team.

• Start engaging potential clients even before your cards and quote forms arrive.

• When the quote forms and cards get to you, practice with a friend (or alone if need be).

• As a practice, use your home as though you have just arrived at someone's house and walk through talking to the potential client and filling out the form.

• Make sure to obtain and enter all of the customer's information legibly, including:

- Their name

- Street address

- City, State

- Zip code

- Phone number

Yes, a million times yes, you want this information. Why? Because if you practice good follow up and maintain contact with your clients, it pays off. You can even send out fliers about 'What's New' (i.e., we now do windows, or carpet cleaning, or dog walking or house sitting). How about a Christmas card list or any major holiday list, or a birthday card list? Clients LOVE this stuff, not to mention it makes your loyal, hard earned clients much tougher for the competition to steal. I doubt you want to go through all the weeding out process only for some new kid on the block to come along with a cute car and a low price and steal your best customers.

Guard your clients like a rabid dog. The genuine ones are hard to come by. Always follow up and never take your customers for granted. They are not your buddies; they are your hard earned clients that make it possible for you to pay your bills and have a nice life. Do not take advantage of them. Be professional, do your job, but keep in constant contact, and never forget their dog or cat. You can let them cry on you every once in a while but do not cry for them. Get a therapist, but keep your personal life private.

Remember: shower, shave, great teeth, clean car, dress professionally. Be awesome, but watch your mouth. Do not make excuses and always be on time. I was successful because I took my advice. It is nearly impossible to win back a client that you have insulted either with your tardiness, sloppy work, or too much mouth.

Chapter 12: Residential Cleaning

General Scope of Work

Common jobs of a general cleaning include cleaning the kitchen and laundry rooms, countertops, sinks, microwave inside and out, removing trash and replacing liners.

General Cleaning Procedures:

- Wipe any drips from cabinet front at the sink area.

- Wash and dry stove top and stove dials.

- Clean table and check seats of chairs for food particles — remove as needed.

- Counters — remove all items from the counter top (do not just scoot them around); Clean and dry counter, then replace items.

- Place dishes in the dishwasher when a dishwasher is present.

- Bathrooms — clean tubs or showers by scrubbing walls as well as the floors of showers.

- Clean countertops including sinks, clean and disinfect toilets, clean mirrors, remove trash and replace the liner in a can.

- When you clean tubs and showers, make sure to — remove all shampoo bottles and clean underneath them, dry the area and then replace the bottles. Similarly, remove the soap from its holder, again clean and dry, then replace.

- Vacuum all the hard flooring and carpeted flooring throughout the home.

- Mop all tile floors throughout.

- Hardwood floors — use a hardwood floor cleaner and the proper mop.

- Vacuum all area rugs, shake small rugs, and replace after floor mopping.

- Vacuum under as many tables and edges of furniture as you can without moving heavy furniture.

- Always move chairs at dining areas to vacuum.

- Dust all furniture including table lamps and ceiling fans. Throughout home use a dusting spray like Endust, does not include the interior of china cabinets.

- Feather dust paintings and their frames.

- Use a product like Windex for glass-topped tables.

- Broom-sweep the front door exterior landing or stoop.

Chapter 13: Moneymakers

Every house has a treasure trove of gritty goodies, including:

- Refrigerators: These tombs of food waste are usually cleaned for approximately twenty-five to thirty-five dollars each.

- Ovens are thirty-five to fifty dollars. The average is forty dollars.

- Grills need to be priced accordingly. They are the equivalent of a disastrous oven and their price should always be higher than their cousin appliance.

- Fronts of all cabinets in the kitchen can vary in level of grime — price out according to the time you think they will take.

- Interior of kitchen cabinets similarly needs to be priced out according to time, but remember that all of the dishes and pans will need to be removed and replaced. Figure this time before pricing. If the homeowner says they will remove the dishes and replace, put this on the quote form — I have priced this out only to arrive, and the cabinets are full. She is standing there with a check made out for the quote. Pay attention and review the paperwork. Same goes for bathroom cabinets and closet shelving.

- Make sure that when you price out her house, you mention dirty dishes. A sink full of dirty dishes can easily add thirty minutes to your time. If she wants dishes washed by hand, that is fine, but she needs to pay for it, like everything else.

Fill out that quotation paperwork with detailed notes!!!

- How dirty are the windows? Also, how hard is it to arrange the screens out?

This is another one to watch out for; if she says her husband is taking out the screens, do the paperwork. If he is taking the screens out, do they still want the Pay attention cleaned? Replaced by you? Is the windows one big window or are they those little tiny ones? The small French-style windows are at least double the cleaning work, price accordingly. Add all of these factors into the price. So if the same six windows without screens are French, charge as if you are doing screens: $70.00-$80.00. Here are some examples of how to the cabinets your window pricing:

Six windows without screens cleaned: $45.00

Six windows with screens cleaned and window tracks: $70.00

Same windows on the second floor without screens: $90.00

Same windows on the second floor with screens and window tracks: $140.00

• Important: if you ever see a broken screen or window report it before you clean or you could end up paying to replace it. Inspect closet shelving carefully when you are walking around to create your quote. The same goes for windows that do not open and close properly. Check these things during your walk-through.

• China cabinets, large libraries, garages, pool decks or pool furniture are other spaces that may require cleaning.

• Wash and dry all the baseboards and doors, crown molding.

• Blinds and shutters need dusting along with vacuuming drapes.

- Chandeliers may need cleaning or any hanging light fixture whether inside or out.

- Laundry and bed changing — if they want the beds changed and remade on each trip, figure it into your costs. HOWEVER, do they have a change of sheets for each bed? If they do, do they want you to wash and dry the dirty sheets? This can be sticky as you might be finished cleaning and you are standing there waiting for the washer and dryer. Negotiate: you change the beds, you throw the sheets in the washer and the homeowner completes the process, OR they can pay you to stand there and watch the machines. Again, when in doubt, put it in your quote!

- Removing trash from homes that people have moved out of can be another lucrative money maker.

- Figure in the extra cost of your trash bags, as well as possible trips to the landfill. We have had truckloads that needed to be removed. Think carefully how many trips and all the extra work in just bagging up the trash, before you can even get to the cleaning.

- You can also try to sell 'tidying up the front garden' for homes that are empty.

Chapter 14: Pets

Pets can increase your cleaning time by hours if the homeowner wants the furniture vacuumed, so price your work accordingly. Spend time documenting their needs. If you priced out a home and the next thing you know they have adopted a dog or cat, your workload is about to increase.

Pet hair takes extra time to vacuum and destroys the air quality of a vacuum cleaner. If you have been using your vacuum cleaner, this can be a real problem. You will need to go to the client and let them know that you can no longer use your vacuum cleaner to vacuum their home (unless you have two, then reserve one for people with pets). The odor of someone's pet being spewed by your vacuum cleaner is not one that will be tolerated by clients that do not have pets.

People that have pets must also supply their mops, as the hair and the occasional messy clean up cannot be dragged into other peoples' homes. If you have been supplying equipment, you can either sell the mops back to the homeowner or use theirs. Do not use mops that have cleaned up pet hair and pet accidents in others homes. It is a poor business practice and will cause unhappy clients.

You would not believe the number of people that allow pets to use their carpets as though they were in the backyard, but it does happen. I personally rid myself of these filthy clients. If you have a tolerance for cleaning up these types of gross disasters, do us both a favor and charge for this.

Chapter 15: Supplying Tools

Keeping your most basic tools with you at all times and organized will make your job easier and much less stressful. I've provided a list of what we needed on a daily basis as well as those items that are just wonderful to have on hand.

A good quality commercial vacuum cleaner is a must — it is expensive, but the home models have plastic fan blades, and with one penny or paperclip, your vacuum is finished. Good commercial vacuums have metal fan blades, and you can suck up nails (no kidding). Go to a janitorial supply store, or shop online if you do not have a reputable source for supplies locally.

Mops and buckets are needed for tile floors. You can use smaller mops that you wring by hand. Do not share mops for tile and wood, since the cleaning chemicals for tile will damage a wood floor. For wet mops, keep a plastic bag in your vehicle to slide the wet mop head into. This will save your vehicle's carpet from stains and odor.

For hardwood floor mops and cleaners, Home Depot is a good start for supplies. The mops for wooden floors have a large rectangular shaped head and a terry cloth cover. They do not look like conventional wet mops. READ the instructions on the hardwood floor cleaner bottle, and please follow them closely.

The best hardwood floor cleaner, in my opinion, is called Bona, and it is not usually found at Home Depot, but is available where carpet and flooring are sold. You can also check Ace Hardware.

For brooms and dust pans, make sure to buy an angled broom and dust pans with nice tall handles. These details save a lot of bending over.

Learn how to use a squeegee. A squeegee will save you a small fortune in paper towels and produce a streak-free pro job on windows and bath mirrors, as well as shower doors and walls. Buy a squeegee that allows the rubbers to be changed easily. Go online to find a supplier unless you have a janitorial supply store nearby.

Other supplies include:

- Long duster to dust ceiling fans.

- Feather duster for artwork and frames.

- Good dusting cloths.

- Scrubbing pads that will not scratch.

- Towels and rags — make sure you launder every day to remove germs and discard when worn.

- Bucket(s) with sturdy handles.

- Small, sturdy ladder — it's your backside, so do not buy junk!

- A tote to hold your cleaning chemicals.

- A colorful bag to hold your clean rags.

- A plastic tote with dividers can hold small hand tools and other items that tend to get damp separate from items such as vacuum cleaner bags that dampness can ruin.

- A plastic scrub brush or two.

- Rubber gloves — both lightweight disposable ones and heavier gloves that you can reuse.

- A regular and a Phillips screwdriver for window screens.

- Spare vacuum cleaner bags and filters — you should keep these with you.

Check the local discount stores as well as office supply stores to see what's available. It's also a good idea to find a storage option that you can easily lift into and out of your vehicle as your work vehicle may also be the family car.

Chapter 16: Supplying Chemicals

• The neutral cleaner is needed for mopping ceramic tile and vinyl. You can also use this on a laminate floor (or a fake wood floor, make sure it is fake).

• A disinfectant spray for the bathroom — Dow bathroom cleaner works great for soap scum, Wal-Mart has a store brand that works nicely as well and is much cheaper. However, I don't care for the fragrance it emits.

• Some bleach in a spray bottle for shower corners — keep this is in a large Ziploc bag as it can ruin your car if it spills or drips. Bleach is extremely corrosive, so keep your vehicle safe from its effects!

- Windex or a similar product is required for cleaning glass surfaces.

- Toilet bowl cleaner — use each client's brush — do not take the brush from house to house! Again, keep this cleaner from spilling in your vehicle, it is very corrosive.

- Endust or a similar is required for dusting furniture. Use Pledge furniture polish, but only if the customer allows as it is oil based.

- 409 or Fantastic spray cleaner or similar for grease cleanup under kitchen hoods, on counters, and cabinet fronts. Do not use on real wood cabinets.

• Disposable gloves — make certain you have a pair of sturdy Playtex gloves and keep a box of disposables with you. Latex free disposables are available if you're allergic. You will thank me when you get into some of those bathrooms.

• Dust masks are very handy to have for homes that you are cleaning for the first time and ones that have pets and dander.

• Use stainless steel cleaner and shiner on stainless steel appliances or for shining a dry stainless steel sink. Try this on Formica cabinet doors, especially dark colored ones.

- Of course, dish liquid like Dawn or something similar would be needed for cleaning dishes.

- Murphy's Oil soap is a good general purpose cleaner and most people like the scent.

- Simple Green is another general cleaner than many people like.

- I never use air fresheners because there are so many those are allergies inducing.

- Paper towels — if you practice with your squeegee the only thing you will need paper towels for will be glass- topped tables. The squeegee is a real money saver.

- A trash bag or two — there will be times when you will clean homes that are getting ready to be sold or people will be moving into. When this happens, do not use the garbage cans but remove garbage to a landfill or other approved location (no one is coming back as it's for sale or vacant).

Do not place anything in the garbage cans!

Chapter 17: Green Cleaning   Thoughts

There are many fine quality green cleaners out there, and I have tried them all. The ones I own had the greatest luck with are the neutrals for floor mopping and the floor waxes. Sadly, I have not found a degreaser that will do a thorough job on anything in the kitchen. However, I can tell you that manufacturers are working on this concept and I think that is great and I am glad to hear it.

So, if you get a client that insists that you 'go green' in their house, use what the market currently offers. I would use the products they have on hand, and I also would not guarantee that you can get all of the soap build up off the shower walls or the grease splatters off the kitchen surfaces. I have cleaned thousands of homes and apartments and, as I said, the chemistry is just not there yet in these green products.

Do respect your clients' wishes, and these are their homes after all. Do the best you can with the products they supply. I have always made sure my customers end up happy. I would be the one who felt like things just weren't clean enough, but to these clients, the lack of harsh chemicals in their home is all important. Again, respect their wishes. I hope we soon see the day where green cuts grime as good as the industry standard.

Chapter 18: Basic Office Needs

Getting started requires organization and a shoebox full of receipts dropped on your accountant's desk in December do not qualify as organized. Purchase a filing cabinet and a package of file folders. My greatest concern is that you have files that track your sales, your customers, stores your receipts, and offers organization to your new business.

You want to be able to make sense of what you are doing and a filing system is a simple but necessary step in the process. You may want to consider taking a basic bookkeeping class such as QuickBooks from your local high school if they offer it. You can also take a class online fairly inexpensively. Your accountant will love you and may even buy you lunch.

Here are some files that you will want to create right away:

- Bank statements

- Credit card receipts

- Cash receipts

- Office supplies

- Cleaning supplies

-

- Business insurance (both workmen's comp and general liability)

- Auto expense insurance

- Auto repairs

- Payroll service

- Sales taxes

- Intangible taxes

- Accountant

- Phone a) cell phone b) land line and fax line c) internet - connection

- Rent on office

- Utilities for office a) electric b) water, sewer, trash

- Equipment inventory — this one is critical since hand tools have a way of coming up missing

You will notice that I did not include items like staplers, pencils, and tape dispensers. Scour garage sales if you need this stuff.

If you keep a log of each employee that checked out a piece of equipment you may quickly recognize which of your employees is always leaving tools behind, bringing tools back in a dirty and damaged condition. I also recommend keeping a log of disposable equipment such as vacuum cleaner bags, vacuum cleaner belts, filters, squeegee rubbers and even general cleaners.

After employing multitudes of individuals, I soon discovered that it is always one or two individuals that lose equipment, damage equipment, leave company vehicles with lunch trash, and other unsavory habits. Maintaining a log will reveal the wasteful, destructive staff members and allow you to make a quick decision regarding their job retention.

One bad apple can disrupt an effective team.

Conclusion

You are licensed, insured, you have your Inc. set up, your federal ID number, a new business checking and a phone. Great! But, there are some other really important aspects of owning any business, and especially in the cleaning business.

First and foremost, I want you to look in the mirror. How are your personal grooming habits? Do you look like you just got out of bed at noon? If you do, I promise you are not going to go far. Cleaning people should have impeccable grooming habits. Your clothes and body should look and smell as if they have experienced meticulous care.

In addition, you should not be advertising Budweiser or any of your other favorite products while you are working. Your uniform should include a plain collared shirt and plain slacks, along with neat and clean covered work shoes should be your uniform. Your company shirts are fine, but not others.

Additionally, how is your dental hygiene? Get dental work if you need it. Bad teeth and bad breath can lose you customers in the same fashion as showing up in rundown cars. Customers do not want leaked oil left on their drive after you have cleaned their home. Keep in mind that if you cannot take care of yourself or your car, there is no reason why people would want to hire you to look after their home or office.

Your presentation is all important, so before you waste more of your time and money, pass the mirror inspection and make sure your car is clean inside and out even if it is 20 years old. Keep it that way.

Appearance Checklist for Men:

• Maintain showered, shaved, clean and groomed hair.

• Be easy on the aftershave. Many people have allergies to fragrance.

• Brushed and flossed teeth.

• Wear plain, collared (yes, collared) shirt with plain colored trousers that fit properly, pressed if needed.

- We do not want to see your underwear (or crevice) so wear clothing that fits you.

- Clean shoes with socks are required.

- Take care that your vehicle is clean inside and out and mechanically sound.

Appearance Checklist for Ladies:

- Maintain showered, shaved, clean and groomed hair.

- Brushed and flossed teeth.

- Easy on the makeup — if they wanted a circus act for the kids, they would not have hired someone to clean the house. Your makeup should be demure and light colored—you are not the evening entertainment, you are the cleaning staff. Look like it.

• Use little to zero perfume. Many people have allergies, or they dislike the strong fragrance. Remember it smells good to you and maybe your husband, but not the general public. Save it for your private life.

• Your collared (yes, collared) shirt and slacks should be neat and pressed.

• Your clothing should not be tight or revealing, and your cleavage and midriff should not be exposed.

- Clean, closed-toe work related shoes with socks are required. No sandals or flip flops allowed.

- Dangling, loose jewelry is not for the workplace, save it for a well-earned date night.

- Take care that your vehicle is clean inside and out and mechanically sound.

To All:

I cannot believe I have to mention this one either but here goes: your children, your friends, and your boyfriend or girlfriend do not belong in your clients' homes or business. You were hired. You were the one they said could come into their home or office, not your extended circle of friends and family. If the babysitter cancels, you need to find someone else. Taking your sick child to a client's home is NOT an option. It is also not a place for you to visit with friends.

Act like a professional and your business will grow. Conduct yourself like a slob and a streetwalker, and you will attract a certain clientele. Good luck with all that. The habit of foul language is one you should break if need be. You will embarrass yourself and present a distasteful impression. So brush up on your manners, it matters.

A final thing you should keep in mind is that many peoples' homes and offices have surveillance cameras that are not visible, so there is every possibility you are being monitored. Conduct yourself as though you are and all will go well.